FROM PAIN TO PURPOSE

A Bridge Over Troubled Waters

Ms. Liles!
Thank you for your
support! Love Erica Rivers
7/27/19

FROM PAIN TO PURPOSE

A Bridge Over Troubled Waters

Sonja Pinckney Rhodes

ISBN: 9781075788338

The scriptures in this book were taken from the King
James Version - Bible in Public Domain;
New International Version (NIV) Holy Bible, New
International Version®, NIV® Copyright ©1973, 1978,
1984, 2011 by Biblica, Inc.® Used by permission. All rights
reserved worldwide.

For information on the content of this book, email
booksbysonja@gmail.com

WrightStuf Consulting, LLC
www.wrightstuf.com

Printed in the United States of America

One ... Pain

Silence, research says, is one of the deadly killers within many diseases, including the heart that attacks or disrupts the natural flow of your organs. You know, the silent symptoms, silent actions, silent shutdowns, silent brokenness, silent tears are all a part of what happened when my heart was attacked at around age six, as I recall. No, it wasn't that my coronary artery suddenly became blocked, stopping the flow of blood to my heart muscle. It was however, the moment of violation that affected the functionality of my heart. A learned behavior of masking, pretending, covering up, and hiding from what was true to my heart; a sacrifice in fear of protecting that which was evil and poison.

Growing up in a household with both of my parents, Johnny and Mary Pinckney, an older brother, Jonathan, who is the true definition of an older brother, who watched over us, bossed us around and once in a while flexed his muscles to prove he was the oldest and in charge. A bonus brother, Dennis, who is actually my first cousin but he lived with us and lived up to his name, Dennis the Menace. My younger sister, Sherri, is five years under me and was always very protective of me; even today people think she's the oldest. She's very direct; says what she means and means what she says. My father was tall, dark and handsome, as well as a hard worker, good husband and the apple of my eyes. My mother is everything a woman, wife and mother is defined to be with the absence of fear and a heart of love. She ran the household with pride and dignity, and expressed herself without any doubt. That dynamic was customary for me. As small children, our grandparents kept us while my parents worked. This would seem to be the perfect environment to leave us with our grandparents, right? Who better to watch over us, to love us unconditionally, to ensure we were fed and well cared for. Who doesn't love to go to grandma's house? Hugs and kisses, treats and loved on, I can imagine. I was blessed to have my maternal grandparents, Prince and Melvina Michael and my paternal grandmother, Elizabeth Kelly Pinckney, as my paternal grandfather was already deceased. Being that I had amazing parents, you could just imagine how wonderful my grandparents would be. Nevertheless, sharing the same DNA doesn't actually mean the same qualities would flow from generation to generation. That can be a blessing and a curse.

As we grew older, my mother didn't really work and my father didn't require her to work; therefore, she kept the house. When we would get in from school, we focused on homework until my father came home from work. It was like clockwork, as he walked in, my mother was putting his food on the table. By the time he gave his joyful greetings, as he was always happy, and washed his hands, his plate was on the table, fork and knife on the napkin, a glass of water, a slice or two of bread, his Texas Pete and his ketchup were set for him to dine. My father put ketchup and hot sauce on everything, even his lima beans. The food was blessed by my father and we all dined together as a family Sunday through Friday. Saturdays were typical meals, such as fish and red rice or hamburgers and hotdogs. We could not play at the table. We were taught to sit straight up in our chairs, hold the fork correctly, cut our meat, not saw it and drink after we were finished. We didn't have a choice in what we wanted to eat; we ate what was on the plate and did not play over it or complain. Once dinner was over, we washed the dishes immediately and if we wanted to watch television, we had to bathe first.

Saturdays, my mom would be getting up with the chickens. By 8 a.m., she had several loads of clothes washed, and although we had a clothes dryer, we still had to hang the garments on the clothesline. By the time my sister and I were settled in the house, the dog would have snatched the clothes off the line, running around the yard with them. Who had to chase the dog for the items and placed them back on the line? Of course, my sister and I did! Those were actually some of the best days of my life!

Since I'm reminiscing a little, I would like to talk about my father for a second. First, I thought he was the most handsome, charming and intelligent man on earth. We were required to use proper English in our home at all times. If we were caught using a slang, we were advised to get Mr. Webster (dictionary) to look the word up, read its meaning aloud, and give the adjective, verb, etc. form or the word. This may seem to be a simple task, but we were lectured about misusing the King's English for, sometimes, hours. I can hear him telling us; *don't mess up the King's English. Look it up!* This was also the case with school, especially math. Well, he didn't like the new math and would always tell us how to work the problems out the way he learned it in school. He just didn't listen to us when we told him we had to "show our work". Therefore, we would take it to school and get it wrong and he would say the school was backwards and not teaching us anything. He argued about why we had to work the problems out the long way when there was a short cut that would give us the same answer. He believed in using our brains and not working it out on paper all the time. It's funny today, but sitting at the table for hours reviewing back then, wasn't humorous at all. My father was a great man. He gained his heavenly wings July 25, 2014. I think about and miss him every day.

5

Before all of that, I can remember walking into the home of my maternal grandparents when I was a small child; they welcomed us with opened arms. Oh the smell of the cakes, pies and cookies baking by my grandfather, who was a chef, and a big jokester. He would always have a joke to tell then laugh louder than anyone else at his own jokes. He was also a prankster. One evening, they stopped by and my grandfather asked for a glass of water. I don't quite remember how old I was but in grade school. My parents had taught us to place a napkin under the glass when serving. I went to give him the glass of water and he faked me out and pretended to have it, so I let it go. The glass fell to the floor and scared me. I stepped back and screamed. I didn't know what happened but everyone ran towards me and my father picked me up. The bottom of the glass broke with the sharp part upright. I stepped on it and my heel was cut in half. I don't remember how many stitches I incurred but I still have that scar on the bottom of my foot today. My grandfather was very hurt and apologetic about it. He didn't mean it but sometimes things happen to us accidentally that leaves everlasting scars, internally and externally. The pain may become numb but the remaining blemish of what happened and how it made you feel, is a constant reminder of what you've been through, and how God has healed you.

As children, we tend to take some things for granted, such as having the skillfully baked goods at our grasp that my grandfather made free for us but sold to other people. Oh, how I miss the aroma and warmth of those sweet treats today, made with hands full of love and passion for his talent. As I became a teenager, I was not granted the same curfew extension as my peers or what I thought were privileges. I remember calling my grandmother to complain about what my mother wouldn't allow. It didn't change my mother's decision, however; it gave me consolation that my grandmother "had my back". Isn't that what we all want? As we live, move and have our being, we want family, friends and employers to give us positive affirmations; to be supportive of our perspective on our lives, goals, opinions and aspirations. However, be very careful of that two edged sword, because true and authentic relationships are what we should desire, but we know that all things work together for the good... according to Romans 8:28. That means the good, the bad and the ugly relationships. Yes, grandmas are special, but we have a way, as I am a grandmother, of sugar coating for the grandchildren. Aww, the joy they bring as I get those hugs and kisses and to have all types of special treats for them to choose from and special places to take them. I want to love on them, protect them and teach them things they will remember me by to share with their own children one day. Actually, the joy I get when I know they are coming to visit motivates me to fill the pantry and the refrigerator with all the things I know they will ask for. Although, I cannot be with them to keep them from falling and skinning their knees, the hurt of the first friendship or the disappointments that life will bring, I sure wish I could.

Even as I became a young adult, my grandmother was still special to me. It may be because I have her characteristics - looks and attitude. She was sharp, independent, with a great sense of humor, but sassy and bossy at the same time. My grandmother retired from Krispy Kreme. She had learned a few trades from my grandfather that she would impart at the donut shop, such as the turnovers. She actually taught them how to make them, and today, they are still sold in the establishments. When she retired, her manager told her she could visit any Krispy Kreme and get free donuts at any time. Well, she took that literally. Years later, Carl, my ex-husband, Andre' and I were taking her home and as we were about to pass by the Krispy Kreme, she told Carl to stop so she could go in and get donuts. I knew the story and told him not to stop. However, he didn't listen. I sat in the car in amazement as I watched through the window how she walked into the store and went behind the donut counter. The young woman was serving a customer and turned as my grandmother proceeded to get an empty box and fill it with donuts. Carl rushed to the car and told me to come get my grandmother. I refused and reminded him that I told him not to take her inside. A nice man agreed that she should have the donuts since she retired from there, but she wasn't happy that the manager didn't see it that way and allow her to have donuts. She and my grandfather have both transitioned to be with the Lord, but their legacy lives on, in and through me.

It is inevitable that any of us can be protected from life's challenges. We will fall off our bikes, friends will walk away, marriages will end, loved ones will die and we will have to learn how to continue to live based on the good and bad things that we encounter in our lives. Is it fair that family hurt us? Why do people hurt people? We may never know the exact answer to that but sometimes, hurt people, hurt people. Oftentimes, envy motivates bad behavior that becomes infectious when passed on to someone else that is already hurt or has low self-esteem. On the other hand, when I began to experience hurt, I retreated within myself, covered up the hurt, put up a wall and learned how to smile on the outside while hurting on the inside. I never said a mumbling word about the violation and the insults. As the years passed and I harbored those violations, the hurt, and the confusion it brought, I developed a dialogue of secrets that I shared only with God. I would pray and cry out to Him about the things that had happened to me; how it made me feel, apologizing for feeling violated, hurt and confused but looking for peace. Asking God to help me not to be angry or harbor hate… and to forgive me for those feelings, because "I" was violated.

I asked God to help me love those who hurt me, and that I would be loved in return. It was so vitally important for God to know I was sorry about what happened to me and that I wasn't angry with the offenders. I just wanted to be loved and accepted. Although they have transitioned from this side of heaven, I still find myself protecting their names. I wanted to go back to the feelings I spoke of at my grandparent's home; I wanted to go back to the hugs, kisses, love and safety I felt that now appears to be gone; I wanted to go back before what was stolen from me, for it to never return to that precious young 6 year old that even affects me now as an adult. Not even my maternal grandmother could kiss and hug me enough to make me feel whole again. Some things cannot be recovered. It is like breaking the seal on a package and releasing its freshness. It becomes tainted, no matter how it is rewrapped or what preservatives are added. The original masterpiece has been damaged or compromised. It can be imitated but never duplicated.

This is the beginning of learning how to live with brokenness; a broken vessel. How do you learn how to breathe again, trust again, and smile from the inside again? It never leaves you. It becomes a part of you, like recovering from a broken arm. That arm may heal but a change in the weather may cause it to ache until you take a pain pill. What is the pain pill for internal hurt? How do you stop the silent tears from flowing when life continues to throw you lemons? Sure, I had a great family, we went to church, I made good grades, participated in extra curriculum activities, had friends, etc. I learned how to adapt to and cover up my internal wounds. I was just a baby, innocent, happy, free and then my heart was attacked.

It's interesting how we interact with one another and not ever know each other's stories. Not just their address, what classes they are in with you, how talented they play football, sing, dance, who their parents are, but not know the intricacies of that person's character and life. In school, I had friends that told me I was pretty, my hair was long and pretty, I dressed nice but I could never see it. What they did not know was that I put on lip gloss to help me look better (be accepted), I did not speak up because my self-esteem was low (I didn't think what I said mattered), I thought I was too skinny, too dark and not pretty enough. I always thought my friends were more attractive, more talented and more adored. I began to measure myself against them not realizing that God fearfully and wonderfully made me, as well. However, I was seeking for that acceptance because, remember, my heart was infected with lies and deceit. It was not functioning in its full capacity of truth and love. I was operating from brokenness because of the deception and the things that occurred. I was sworn to secrecy so I no longer had a voice. I remember hearing stories of children that did not speak for years then when their silence was broken, they spoke of the injustice that happened to them. I am that child. I may have spoken words, but I suppressed the hurt associated with the act deep inside of me. Not that I ever forgot because I live with it every day of my life. I have learned how to bury the hurt, embarrassment and shame it brought. Therefore, being accepted by my peers was important at that time. I knew I had an amazing family. We lived in a beautiful home, my parents instilled spiritual principles in us, they had a great marriage, and we were well-rounded children. My brother, Jonathan and cousin, Dennis played sports and my sister, Sherri and I were cheerleaders, ballet dancers and ran track. I was the first queen of Forest Park as a cheerleader for the rec football team. I was crowned and the football player was the king. It was like half-time at a game and he escorted me off the field. I believe it may have been a Burger King hat wrapped in foil. So funny but cute! My parents supported every activity from school, to extracurricular and church ministries. It was a typical household with my brother, cousin, my sister, and I, the middle child, whom of course thought I was overlooked. Moreover, that is the generalization of who we are and of my family dynamics.

Even living in such a close and loving household, no one knew my secret. I would often hear my mother on the phone tell someone that she did not know why my self-esteem was so low. She would joke about me putting on lip-gloss just to go outside to check the mailbox. I was always in the mirror. I was frequently called "stuck up". My peers often said I thought I was "cute", but I was actually over-compensating for what I believed was a lack of what I thought I did not possess, which was beauty and inclusion among family and friends.

Here I am in high school, a place of growth and development to prepare for college and the foundation of pursuing professional goals. I made good grades, and was to some of my teachers, the teacher's 'pet' or favorite. Yes, it sounds normal but it was still a struggle of being noticed and fitting in with others. My parents were pretty strict, especially about doing well in school, phone calls and curfews. I was allowed to go out but I had to be in before midnight and not a minute after 11:59pm. I could talk on the phone but not after 9 p.m. If a call came in for me after 9 p.m., my father would make it clear to the caller that Sonja does not receive phone calls after 9 p.m. and if they did not want their feelings hurt or mine, they had better not call after 9 p.m. So embarrassing! But where did those days go?

Fast-forwarding...

My senior year of high school, I met a nice "cute" young man named Greg through a mutual friend. He was in his freshman year at the Citadel Military College and we began to date. We talked on the phone and laughed a lot, as teenagers do, and often hung out for dinner or at the movies. I thought it was pretty cool dating someone in college and in uniform. I would pick him up from campus because freshmen were not allowed to have vehicles. Their curfew, I believe, was midnight, which was my curfew to be in the house, as well. Spring and the end of the school year came around and I was preparing for graduation and my senior prom. The school term was coming to an end for college students, as well. Greg began to ask if I was ready. One date night, we made a detour to a hotel.

Little did I know that my life would change in that instance.

Greg lived out of town, but he promised to come back to take me to my senior prom and he did! He rented a car and came in a tuxedo with a wrist corsage for me. Oh, wow, he showed up and I was escorted by a good-looking college student that lived out of town to my senior prom. I felt pretty special to say the least. I still have my prom picture reminding me of how small in size I was back then, but most of all, the memories of that evening. We continued to stay in touch but because of the distance, we did not see each other as I thought we would. I graduated and began to prepare for college. A few weeks before my departure, I mustered up the nerves to ask my mom if I could have birth control pills. She asked if I was ready for that and I softly said, "just in case". Well, my mother took me to the doctor. I remember the day so clearly. I nervously sat in the waiting room with my mom and Sherri. They called my name and I went back alone. The doctor sat and talked to me for a few minutes before the exam. I told him I was about to leave for college and wanted birth control pills. After the exam, he came back in after I was dressed, sitting there praying to God that I wasn't pregnant. He sat down and calmly said, "Sweetheart, you're a little too late for birth control pills. You're about 12 weeks pregnant."

I immediately began to cry. I didn't know how I was going to keep that news from my parents and how they would react when I told them. He asked if I was alone and I told him that my mom and sister were in the waiting room. He instructed me to go get her and meet him in his office across the hall. I said to him that I was okay and would tell her myself.

He sternly said, "We will tell her", and he instructed me to go get her.

I wiped my tears before opening the door that lead to the waiting room. I said, "Mama, come here."

See, I have one of those mamas that smiles and is sweet as apple pie until you cross her! Then, you're liable of getting tongue lashes that feels like strappings from an explosion. She said okay and walked to the door. We went into the office and the doctor began to explain that he performed my exam and there were no signs of problems; however, the possibility of me receiving birth control pills was not an option at this time because the exam revealed that I am about 12 weeks pregnant. Sometimes, you have to be blunt. This wasn't anything my mom was expecting so she was still sitting pretty with her legs crossed and lips cutely folded in. She listened attentively and nodded her head as in agreement or yes, I understand. So he said it again, "She's too late for birth control pills because she's about 12 weeks pregnant."

Then the realness hit. Mama uncrossed her legs and said, "What?!? Lord, have mercy!"

I was too afraid to look to the left or to the right.

The doctor said, "These things happen and it's important for you to be there for her because she will need your support and will need to start coming in for her regular appointments."

Mother Dear was not happy with me so I sat in the back seat going home. The first thing she did was swiftly toss the papers that were in her hands and said, "Here's your bill!"

I didn't say a single word all the way home.

My father was a vibrant, happy man. As we pulled up to the house, I could see him doing yard work in the front of the house. He was happy to see us. He said, hey and asked, "Where were my girls all day?"

My mom said, "Ask your daughter!"

He laughed and asked again, where we were.

Once again she said, "Ask your daughter!"

Well, this daughter walked straight into the house because she didn't want to be asked. I felt so ashamed, embarrassed and strongly hurt that I had let my parents down. I worked at one of the movie theaters and was happy to go in that day. Needless to say, that canceled my college plans. I had now disappointed my parents and myself. Once again, the shame and embarrassment I felt was enormous. I had made my way through the journey of high school and graduating with an acceptance to college, but yet I failed. I failed my dream, my parents, my hope and myself for the moment. It was the beginning of new beginnings. But are all new beginnings great? Do they come wrapped in pretty paper with a bow?

Beyond the disappointment, I was afraid and depressed. Not only did I go through the pregnancy alone because Greg did not come back, but I was once again rejected, not good enough, not important enough and alone in my feelings in a new journey. I began to retreat again. I took refuge to protect myself. I had to face my family, friends and peers with this lifestyle change I couldn't hide and that I thought would hinder my life from college, achieving my goals and being successful. Then my father sat me down and said to me, "not to worry, he would take care of me and my baby; I was not the first and I won't be the last. This could have been avoided but there's no need to cry over spilled milk because I can still achieve my goals".

Those words of positive affirmation changed my outlook. It did not matter what my friends and family thought of me because my daddy had my back. We must know that not all setbacks are denials and beautiful blessings can be born from hurtful places.

Greg enlisted in the U.S. Army and I didn't hear from him during boot camp. He had promised to come see me before he went in but he didn't. I remember staying in the bed all morning the day he went in because he didn't come. After my son, Jon, was born I called his mother's house and was told about his graduation date from boot camp. Dennis and I went and to my surprise he had a girlfriend there. He acted as though nothing was wrong. He took Jon and said to her, here's my offspring... really? I didn't hear from him after that for about a year. We began to talk on the phone regularly, and he came to see Jon once or twice. We talked about getting married and made plans for me to meet him at his parent's home in Columbia, SC. I knew his family and was welcomed. We talked about me going to Alabama where he was stationed for about a week then come back and get married. Well, while I was at the parent's a young lady that I had never met was there. I asked him who she was and he said just somebody. I went inside to feed Jon and she walked in the house. We greeted each other and I asked if she wanted something to eat. She said, no then asked who I

22

was to Greg. I looked down at Jon on my lap and asked why. She said because she is Mrs. Free, they got married and he was keeping it a secret from everyone. His parents and siblings didn't even know. She began to cry and I hugged her and told her not to cry. I went outside and asked him if it was true and he ignored me. I left and went home distraught, confused and angry. I can count the number of times on one hand that he visited Jon his entire life.

During the pregnancy, I began to have nightmares. Yes, about the things I thought I had buried. I was not sure why the new life inside of me was causing that old stuff to come out. It is like putting new wine into old bottles. The two cannot co-exist. Transformation was taking place inside of me. New birth was giving life to my old situation and making room for my new beginning. Some of the most beautiful things are birthed out of pain. The process is not comfortable, easy or simple. I would awaken in tears and unable to fall back to sleep. I would talk to the Lord through my agony then get up in the morning, put my mask on and go about my day. That is all I knew to hide the pain.

23

However, one night I could not keep it to myself. I needed my mother. I had to tell her what I was going through and what I had been through for the past twelve years. How I made it through school, how I kept a smile on my face, how I went to that house over and over again knowing the things that happened there, reliving it in my mind, looking them in their faces and keeping the secret of what they had done to me. It is the core reason I think I do not have a voice to be heard, the reason I have allowed certain things to happen to me, and the cycle I just could not get out of that haunted and taunted me into my adult life.

I spilled some of it late that night to my mom. I was afraid of hurting her; afraid that she would look at me differently, afraid that she would be angry with me for "allowing" this heinous thing to happen to me. See, when we are violated, we somehow let the enemy trick us to think we are responsible. He tells us that if we say anything, we would get in trouble with our parents. He makes us feel that we are insignificant, that we are not enough, or something terrible would happen to us if we speak up. Therefore, we keep our mouths shut and begin to live in fear of something we did not do but manipulated into thinking we did or deserved. It's not normal and it's wrong. I say us and we because I'm speaking to everyone that has been violated. You are not alone. The snake is cunning. Jesus says it best in John 10:10 that the thief comes not, but for to steal and kill and destroy. Then He says that He came that we might have life and we might have it more abundantly. Knowledge is power and confession is good for the soul.

Confession ...

The illusion of darkness, even in the mind, is the fear of light. Exposure for me at the point of telling my mother was being heard and being seen; revealing my nakedness. Something I thought I was not worthy of or that I did not possess; that is to be seen and heard. Understand, my parents and family had told me frequently that I was pretty and smart. My mom often encouraged me to be more outspoken in church, as I grew older. She always told me that I was a good speaker. Take note that when someone says something to you, even at a young age, which speaks to your spirit, it is confirming what God has already placed inside of you. However, we can be told and shown but until it is believed in the heart that we are all the things that God created us to be, we are not truly living abundantly - on purpose. We often let fear stop us from receiving our gifts by believing the lies of the enemy. Thus, I knew it was truth but apprehension kept me from acknowledging, living, believing and moving forward in those affirmations. It was all a part of protecting my image. I did not want to look broken. I wanted to appear happy and thriving even in the presence of my mother, who embraced and mourned with me. I had been hiding it all this time when the one person that gave birth to me was right there all along to comfort and walk me through this process. That is the perfect solution, right? Let's see, if I had relied on my parents, they could have confronted the situation and I could have avoided the pain of revisiting that place and those people, then consequences for their actions would have taken place. More hurt on top of hurt would have occurred. Yes, speak up and be heard. Nevertheless, I now know that it was a time for me to take refuge in the Lord… a time for me to declare what happened to me and how I felt. I cried on my knees in prayer many nights asking God to forgive me, asking Him to help me not feel that way; help me to love those who hurt me and that they would love me back, and help me to forget because I still felt the fear, the anxiety, the shame, the confusion and the hurt. God comforted me and strengthened me. Did it go away? No, it was still inside of me but I learned how to cope and deal effectively with those difficult things. Now, not only did God know but also my mother knew the surface of things. She did not know the how and why it was permitted.

Exposure …

I had the privilege of having two living grandmothers. My paternal grandmother was tall, light-skinned with long beautiful hair. I remember her grits smothered with chicken or turkey and gravy for breakfast and brown farm eggs. She loved to watch soap operas, *The Young and the Restless*, *The Guiding*

Light and *As the World Turns*. I remember her laugher but not much warmth towards me, as I recall as a little girl. My first cousins and I would enjoy playing on the park with strict instructions not to go on Cracky Street. It was like saying, go on Cracky Street. Grandma would have *something* waiting for us as soon as we got to the door scolding us for disobeying her.

There was a rocking chair in my grandmother's living room that my uncle Leon sat in and rocked back and forth in all day long, talking to the actors on the television screen and laughing out loud. He was diagnosed with schizophrenia. I was never really comfortable around him and would be careful in his presence, which meant I did not feel safe. I recall him taking baths with the bathroom door opened and walking out completely naked having a conversation with my grandmother in my presence and she would say to him, "Go put on some clothes".

He wouldn't listen. He would keep standing there talking to her. One day, he came from his bedroom and asked me to come to his room to listen to music. I shook my head no and he continued to beckon for me to come. I would not move but my grandmother sternly said, "Oh, go on! He just wants you to listen to music."

I remember getting up slowly and walking behind him, through the front bedroom, turning left onto the hallway passing the bathroom, and through the kitchen. His bedroom was right off the kitchen. He closed the door and turned on, what I remember to be, a wooden box radio that was on his dresser or table. He sat on his bed and I stood near the door. He told me to come to him. I was afraid to not move and afraid to move. I had never been in his room alone with him with the door closed. No one could hear me. I was too far away from the front room. I was hoping my grandmother would come get me or tell him to open the door. I walked slowly over to him. Remember, he was mentally ill so his teeth were decayed and his hair was outgrown and unkempt. He began to talked to himself and laugh aloud. I do not know why I did not run or yell for my grandmother to come get me. Then I heard her in the kitchen. I was so relieved because I knew she would open the door to see about me. I can hear her moving about at the sink and I am anticipating her opening the door. I can now hear her footsteps but it begins to disappear. Once again, I am left alone. He lies on his back with his legs hanging on the side of the bed as I stood there. Seconds seemed like minutes and minutes felt like hours. The time must have stopped. Then he gets up and stands in front of me. He begins to say things and ask me questions that I do not comprehend or remember because of fear. I did not answer. He commences to remove his pants and underwear then lies on his back again. I am afraid to look, move or yell for my grandmother. In my young mind, grandmothers are to protect, love and nurture. My parents would have never allowed me to be enclosed with anyone and if noticed, the door would have been opened asking, why the door is closed? My mind is wondering, where is my grandmother? I looked back at the door but I can't move. Why is she not rescuing me? How could she not be concerned about that door being closed, I'm now wondering. He begins to touch himself. He called me to him. I understood but I don't remember how and when I moved toward the bed or suddenly stopped. He tells me again to come to him reaching his hand out for me. I walked closer but didn't reach for his hand. He opens his legs for me to stand in front of him and I can see him look up at me. He continues to caress himself while I'm standing there. I don't know what to do. Then he tells me to touch and I would not. I knew nakedness but not a man's nakedness, as I was only about six years old. I knew it was wrong and I should not be in there with him undressed. He pulled my small fragile hands and placed it on his genitals. He told me to touch it. He moves down closer to the edge of the bed for me to reach. He then guides my hands with his hand to rub it. He rest back for a while with his hands on mine as I stood there afraid and confused, not knowing what I was doing, and why I was touching him. He is talking but I don't know what he is saying. He sits up and tells me to take my panties off and come on the bed. Listen, I am a baby! Why is this man telling me to do this? He touched me, and I remember him saying, let me see. He then tells me to lie on top of him. Now, I am not just afraid of him or what's happening, but afraid of getting in trouble with my grandmother if she walked in because the damage has already been done. It was too late to save me. I am talking about exposure to darkness. A time that my light of innocence is dimmed, a painful memory that would be embedded forever, and a shame that moves emotion because I cannot take it back, rewind, erase or have the opportunity to do it over and claim my voice. How is that done with the person I must have respect for, demands me to go to a dangerous place to be burned by fire, then not nurture my wounds?

I vaguely remember laying on him, I do not remember getting up or getting dressed and I do not understand if there was penetration. I do not remember walking from his bedroom to the front room but I do remember shamefully crossing the threshold of the living room. The question was never asked, was I hungry, or what I was doing in the room or why was I back there so long or did I take a nap? It may have seemed like I was back there forever, in my mind, but maybe it wasn't; giving my grandmother the benefit of the doubt. I was afraid that my grandmother would ask the right question, but she didn't ask any questions. I eased down on the sofa and couldn't look at her. I knew something happened that should not have happened and it was the beginning of happenings. He continued to ask me to come listen to music and told me that I better not tell anyone.

Two

Ever since that day, I have never felt secure, or comfortable at my grandmother's or in my uncle's presence. I never wanted to go there anymore but I didn't want to hurt my dad's feelings that I didn't want to go to his mother's house. Although, I did not harbor feelings of hate or anger, even as I grew into a young adult, I yearned for the affirmation of my grandmother's love, affection and acceptance that a grandmother gives to her grandchildren. I did not ask the question, *why did this happened to me*, but I sure did ask God why she did not love me. This may seem small, but when imparted to a child, it can sometimes set the tone of how we view ourselves. See, these things never left me. It took the innocent joy of being a child away because I now had a fear and apprehension of going to my grandmother's house. I was afraid to see my uncle and of him telling my parents about the secret. I did not have a pack with him, but I did have a threat not to tell anyone. How does a six year old fully understand why they should keep anything from their parents? Seems to be a bit uncommon, right? You see, my parents were amazing. We had everything we needed. My mother prepared dinner every day, the good manners was expected from us, as well as keeping our bedrooms cleaned and the responsibility of having chores around the house that did not yield paid allowances. We attended church and Sunday school just about every Sunday. My father was a firm yet gentle man. I called him a gentle giant. He was happy all the time, loved life and loved people even the more. He was big in stature and strong in his beliefs, but his yea was his yea and his nay was his nay and he meant what he said. That means, we were told once to behave or settle down and he kept his word. Our home was not short of love and laughter. Oh, and my mother still cooks the best meals. There is nothing like mama's cooking. I still cannot complement the way she kept a home, heard my thoughts when I wanted to talk back but dared not to, and that stern look that meant, *I can't get to you now, but I will later* while in the church choir. Although we did not have to say yes ma'am or sir, we had to use proper English, and no slangs, unless we wanted to retrieve *good ole* Mr. Webster from the bookshelf for the correct pronunciation and meaning of the appropriate word.

How do you keep a secret from your security blanket - the ones who took excellent care of you, fed you, provided and protected you? You can't! My mother knew something was wrong but could not put her finger on it... the ultimate "cover up". Suppression, defeat, withholding, restriction, concealment, arrest and repression are all the same forms of "cover up". It is being imprisoned in your own mind and having the knowledge that what you know is so powerful, that it would be life-changing, bring destruction and create a hostile environment. Proverbs 16:18 says, "Pride goes before destruction and a haughty spirit before a fall". What does that actually mean? Proud people take little account of their weaknesses and do not anticipate stumbling blocks. They think they are above frailties and can escape judgement. There is an old adage that says, *what's done in the dark, will come to light.* I trust God's Word that He will make our enemies our footstools. As I look back over my life, I can truly see how that was the case in this situation. I may not have seen a fall or destruction with my physical eyes, but what I do realize as a mature adult is that they did not live their best lives.

I understand that when people do things or try to harm you, it is a form of prejudice. They have a sense of superiority and believe you are inferior to them. They also feel they have the power to control you because of their position and/or role they play in your life. This is motivated because of fear that you have the ability to become or possess greatness. However, they know that you have not arrived at that understanding yet, so they try to damage and distort the obvious good in you that they see. The root of it is envy, jealousy and resentment. One thing for sure, I was loved and adored by my parents. I was a well-spoken toddler, and well mannered. I walked at eight-months old and was weaned from the bottle at nine-months. I was accepted into a two-year old program at the YWCA at 18 months old because I could feed myself and I was potty-trained. See, God's hands were already on me. I was already blessed and favored. This tragedy did not break me. It made me stronger and a better person. 2 Corinthians 4:8-9 says we are troubled on every side, yet not distressed; we are perplexed, but not despair, persecuted, but not forsaken, cast down, but not destroyed. What the enemy meant for evil, God made good. My life was already predestined but the journey was tough. Hindsight is truly 20/20. If I only knew then what I know now, right! But, I would not be who I am today.

I am always working at improving myself to be a better person to serve others. Why? Because when a person is violated, they become isolated in their minds. It brings a sense of worthlessness, embarrassment and disgrace. Their heads may not be held down but their hearts are. For me, I lost my voice. I felt like I wasn't heard and I was afraid to speak. I felt that what other people said was more important than what I had to say. I was told not to say anything, so I felt like I just didn't matter, and that people could mistreat, disgrace and disregard me and there would be no consequences for their actions. The hurtful part is that it was my family who dishonored me, therefore, I not only freely loved and shown honor, I had no choice but to respect the home and the people in which I was left to care for me. Speaking as a 6-year old: As for my uncle, although mentally ill, I believe he understood what he was doing and that it was okay to ask me to his room in the presence of my grandmother. He realized that there were no consequences. Meaning, I wasn't of any value or concern that would demand an after-effect of his actions. I could make so many excuses for them both. Speaking as a young child, again: Maybe, he was not in his right mind; maybe, she was afraid of him; maybe she believed we were truly listening to the radio with his door closed for an unknown length of time, but remember, I was left with my blood relative to care for me and keep me safe from harm and danger to the best of her ability. Maybe she didn't have anyone to nurture her as a child. Maybe the same thing happened to her. As I've said, hurt people, hurt people. I'm not sure if I reminded her of someone that wasn't nice to her, neglected or rejected her. These are questions that have haunted me all my life and I will never know the answers, but it opened the door for wishful thinking. I wished my grandmother loved me. I wished she was nice to me. I wished she hugged me. My immature mind could not process the devastation of what happened to me at that young age. That was the moment I lost my identity. Temporarily. Who was I, how do I even explain what just happened, how do I get back to that safe place? It's like the moment that Adam and Eve realized they were naked after they had taken a bite of the forbidden fruit. I was afraid. There was no rescue, no do overs, no trust and no covering.

According to Webster, identity crisis is a period of uncertainty and confusion in which a person's sense of identity becomes insecure, typically due to a change in their expected aims or role in society. How could a six-year-old have an identity crisis? In most cases, they are not old enough to know their purpose in life; how to obtain their goals and who they actually are besides a happy and carefree child. While that is true, I see my sister as a toddler sitting on my grandmother's lap dipping toast in her coffee cup. I watch as my grandmother played with her and listened to her cynically say to my sister, none for Sonja, only me and you, as I sat and looked at how she loved on my sister, I longed for the same thing. I remember the feeling of being uncomfortable, but I dared not think about being disrespectful by speaking or even asking for some. It was difficult looking at her when she was saying it, as I felt the exclusion of love and attention, and paralyzed in my voice. My sister and I were too young to understand that small act of disregard. Disapproval at such a level led to threats and verbal abuse. I often wondered if she often cunningly used my sister to get next to me to make me jealous and to feel left out. Even as my sister sat on her lap, my grandmother would give her positive affirmations of how pretty she was and how black and ugly I was. I can still hear her saying, you're pretty and she's black and ugly. Those are words that I have never been able to etch out of my head. Talking about a self-esteem issue, I have at this point been sexually abused by my mentally ill uncle, ignored by my grandmother who had no concern for me in that room, excluded from love and affection and now told that because of the color of my skin, that I am unattractive. Whoa! I, as an adult, still cannot fathom, understand or process that type of love. Oh, the hurt I still feel just disclosing that information. Legions attached themselves to me named unworthiness, unimportant and ugly. I am still fighting those weak demons, but on my knees. I have learned how to speak life into my situation that I am more than a conqueror through Christ Jesus who loves me. I am fearfully and wonderfully made. I am above and not beneath. No weapon that is formed against me shall prosper and my comings and goings are blessed.

Three

My mother was a jack-of-all-trades but one of her best crafts, as a licensed cosmetologist, was doing our hair. My mom would put such a hard pressing on our hair that it lasted two weeks until it was time to do it all again. Before dropping us off to my paternal grandmother's house, she would tell me to brush my sister's hair after we were dressed. She kept us well groomed. People would always say that we didn't have a strand of hair out of place. I was the big sister and I proudly followed my mother's directive. We would get dressed and as we sat on the enclosed porch or the entrance through the front door of the house, I would brush my sister's hair. She would squirm sometimes and my grandmother would spank, chastise and warn me not to let her catch me doing her like that again. Thinking I was doing a good thing; something my mother told me to do, but I got bum rushed like a Medea! I became pretty crafty with braiding, so after my mother shampooed our hair, she would ask me to cornrow my sister's hair. I was good at it so it was my job every two weeks. I recall my paternal grandmother's beauty and her long pretty natural hair. One evening my parents, siblings and I were at her house and my grandmother asked my sister to do the two-braid style to her hair. We used to call this Indian style braids with a part in the center and a cornrow braid on each side. My sister did not know how to braid, and probably still does not, so my father told me to do it. As I began to approach her, she shunned and pushed me away saying she asked Sherri to do it. As I slowly backed away to return to my seat, my father, not knowing the history of how my grandmother mistreated me over the years, spoke up and told her to let me braid her hair because Sherri didn't know how. She reluctantly conceded but was not happy about it. I was aware of it. I felt it in her posture and her spirit, but I never said anything to anyone because I wanted to braid her hair so she could be proud of me.

I was about seventeen then. I don't think she told me thank you, but I was proud of my craft and wanted her to like it. I knew she didn't want me to touch her and as I sat down and looked at her, it triggered that same feeling of dissatisfaction and disregard that happened to me as a child, and that feeling often occurs today. Still, I dismiss it when people do it to me because that's what I learned as a child. It makes me wonder why people think it is okay to treat someone less than the way they deserve to be treated and have a haughty spirit about it. I recall what my father would say; when people think they are better than you are, when they talk negatively to and about you, it is often triggered by jealously or envy. How can a person think he or she is better than you are and be jealous? Those who are confident in themselves believe in self-importance. Therefore, they recognize the humble spirit in others, as well as the spiritual confidence in others that comes only from God. When we are weak, He is strong and although people think they are getting away with things, God sees it all and confirms it in His Word that says, "Vengeance belongs to Him". We must continue to walk in love. God has given me self-control. I do not react immediately; I retreat to pray for God's guidance. Others may see this as a weakness, but I am exercising in the power of God to step back and evaluate the situation before responding. However, it's a weakness if you become a doormat and allow people to walk over and talk over you. Death and life are in the power of the tongue (Proverbs 18:21). Whoever said that sticks and stones may break your bones but names will never hurt you did not realize the power of words that cuts like a double-edged sword. Words have favorable and unfavorable consequences that sometimes leave a lifetime of permanent scars. The stigma of my paternal grandmother's words still tries to haunt me as though I am still that little girl trapped inside of my body waiting to be rescued. Ever needed a do-over and wondered what the outcome would be? Maybe, I would not be sensitive to the hurt in someone else's spirit or not give positive affirmations to let others know how special they are, or more open to share the powerful gifts that God has blessed me with if I was not desecrated.

As the Apostle Paul advised in Philippians, we must press toward the mark for the prize of the high calling of God in Christ Jesus. Did God say it would be easy? No, but He promised He would never to leave us nor forsake us. In my midnight hours, I drew nigh to God. I did not know Him like I do today, but I knew He was real, even as a broken child. He kept me and never left me in my times of distress, as the Psalmist said in Psalm 91. He is my fortress, my refuge, my strength and my strong tower, my God in Him I trust. He also gave His angles charge over me! This does not mean I won't get discouraged, disappointed or that I am even free from hurt but I know that as He has delivered me in the past, He will continue to cover, keep and restore my soul. I am really more than a conqueror through Christ Jesus. He gave me a beautiful smile and today my smile radiates from within. The joy that I have, the world didn't give it to me and the world cannot take it away.

Four

You would think that having a wonderful role model of a father, I would make the best choices in relationships. Well, marriage number one was a failure and marriage number two was a duplicate of one. I was not operating in wholeness. I was still a broken and a wounded little girl in this young adult body. Yes, I had accomplished a few things; high school graduation, the birth of a beautiful son, some college and an office job. I did not know what to look for in a relationship besides cute. Oh, cute is important but if you are not partnered with whom God has for you, cute is just the surface. Cute cannot provide, comfort, give protection and support you in all areas of your life where you should thrive as a young married couple. Husband number one, Terry, was tall, easy on the eyes, had an identical twin and was very popular. When we met, he was in high school and I was in middle school. I had this schoolgirl crush on him. He was always nice, and he never disregarded me, although I was below an underclassman. I started riding his bus home in the afternoons and he would take me, and others that were not on his route, home. After he graduated, I started high school but kept in touch with him from time to time; just to say hello. Some years went by and we somehow crossed paths. We began to talk more frequently on the phone. My oldest son was about two years old at this point. Our friendship grew and we began to hang out more often with his twin brother and his wife, family and friends. He met my parents and Terry and I fell in love. I think. The next thing I knew, he proposed to me and I was planning a wedding. My father spent a pretty penny on a very lovely wedding with about 300 guests at a nice hotel, ice sculptures, a beautiful wedding gown, an expensive cake and plated dinner… amazing. It was two lives coming together as one; the perfect complement, you would think.

What we thought was happily ever after soon turned into a disaster. I felt alone, unimportant, abandoned and disappointed. He frequented the club scene (which was never my type of atmosphere) without me just about every weekend. I was never invited to go along and if I asked, my request was declined. I hated for the weekends to come around because he was always gone; sometimes for the entire weekend. He didn't come home after work on some Fridays and I wouldn't see him until Sunday evening or Monday after work. I remember feeling lonely and frustrated. We would often argue because of this and he would stop talking to me for days. I recall one evening wanting to cook something special for him in hopes that it would smooth things out. I couldn't wait to get home so I could prepare the meal and surprise him when he got home from work. When I opened the door, the surprise was on me. As I walked in, I immediately noticed the television was gone but I wanted to secure my house, so I shut and locked the door. Soon I realized that all of the furniture was gone, too. Imagine the shock and confusion. However, my spirit knew I wasn't robbed. I knew he moved all of the furniture out while I was at work. Terry was an entrepreneur so when I called his place of business, his twin brother, answered the telephone. I imagine he knew what was going when he heard my voice on the phone. When Terry came to the phone, he asked, "What," in an angry tone.

I asked the obvious question, if he moved the furniture out. He said yes and told me not to ever call his number again, and then he hung up abruptly. Hysterical and in disbelief, I called my sister-in-law. I imagine, she knew, also. She urged me to call my parents, but I didn't want to. I was too ashamed, confused and embarrassed. After four-months of marriage, I went home to my parents and they welcomed me back. I called out from work the rest of the week and buried myself in tears in my bedroom at my parent's home. I didn't call because he told me not to ever call that number again.

A week passed. Terry called and asked if we could meet to talk. We did, and against my parent's advice, I went back to him. It wasn't long before things were rocky again. He continued in his same pattern and began to make detours after work. I couldn't understand why he never wanted to eat dinner, besides the fact that I was a lousy cook at the time, but then I realized he would eat at his mother's before coming home. One evening, he was in the back of the apartment in our bedroom. I went to ask him what was wrong; why he wasn't talking to me. An argument ensued, and he pushed me against the wall in anger. He put his hands around my neck as he argued back with me, and then released me suddenly. He walked back to the front of the apartment and sat down as though nothing had occurred. I walked up to him and asked if he realized what he had just done. He ignored me as though I wasn't there and something inside of me snapped. I took my fist and punched him on the side of his face. That was the first and only time we ever assaulted one another. I'm not proud of that at all and I never intended that to happen but when you don't walk away in anger, you lose self-control and violence can occur. I was in shock and in fear. I did not have on shoes or a coat on that cold evening. There was no time to think about that. I opened the door and ran for my life. I kept running and running until I knew he was no longer behind me.

A church member, John, who I grew up with, lived in the same complex so I went to his home. I wiped my face and calmed down as much as I could before I knocked on his door. He greeted me with warmth and invited me inside his home. He and his wife, Jackie, asked me how I was doing but I lied and said I was fine. I sat down. Jackie noticed that I was barefoot and asked where my shoes were. I broke down and cried. I could not contain my emotions, so I told them what happened. John was so upset. He suggested that I call my parents, but I didn't. Again, ashamed and humiliated about the state of my marriage and my life, he walked me back home. As we approached my unit, I saw that my car was blocked in by his family and friends. They were standing outside like a gang waiting for little ole me. We walked past them and when I got to my door, they would not let him in. When I entered, his brother and sister began to slander me. I sat on the sofa surrounded by them. I wasn't allowed to leave, move or use the phone. When they all stepped outside of the door, his brother placed his foot at the doorframe so it wouldn't close. After a few minutes, he accidentally moved his foot and I slammed the door shut, locked it and called the police and my family. They all arrived, and a police officer recommended that one of us leave the premises. I never went back except to get my belongings. That was the beginning of the end. At least that's what I thought back then.

I was married for four months! I had plenty of time to wonder what happened to the friendship; to the love. It was lost in the fairytale of it all. What a major setback I had. I was so hurt and disgraced that I did not want to be seen in public. If anyone tells you that it's easy to walk away, that healing is comfortable, it's a lie. I often pondered why I wasn't good enough. Why it did not work? It did not work because it was not ordained by God, but it served a purpose in my life. Little did I know then that it was breaking me, to make me. As I began the long journey of healing and recovery, God was showing me more and more that He knows the plans He has for my life; to prosper me and to be in health (Jeremiah 29:11). I had many weeping nights, but joy was on the way and healing eventually took place. I remained single for about five years before opening my heart again.

Five

During my single period, I focused on raising my son and healing. My career had begun at a local hospital just before my marriage. After the breakup, I started meeting new people and feeling better about myself. I lived with my parents until I saved enough money to get an apartment for my son and me. I was proud of my small accomplishments. I was able to pay my rent, daycare, provide for my son and pay one of the most important things for me - my tithes. As far as I can remember, when I earned wages, I was proud to pay a tenth to God. My parents paid and as I honor my parents, I followed their teachings.

I lived in the apartment until my son was about six or seven years old. Because of my father's job, my parents transferred out of state. Consequently, I moved back into the house where I grew up (until he was reassigned back home). God is so amazing! He gives us new beginnings over and over again.

I met my second husband, Carl, through mutual friends, and we were married within four months. Did I pray about it? I don't remember but I will soon find out, won't I? I was in for a roller coaster ride and my seatbelt was not fastened.

Wow, where do I start? I remember the day we met in the mall parking lot. Our formal introduction. I was not impressed at all. He was slouched in the driver's seat and he looked like he had the weight of the world on his shoulders. I didn't receive much eye contact and there was very little conversation, however, he called me after that encounter, and we became really good phone friends in a very short period of time. He was freshly divorced and living with his brother and family. I was still employed full time at the hospital, and he worked part-time at a restaurant. Ah boy! The next thing I did that I've learned not to do again, was to invite him, a stranger, into my home. Yes, we had mutual friends, but I really didn't know him. The things I endured in eight years were pretty appalling. Yes, we had some great times together but once again I was disrespected, spoken to in a demeaning manner, not supported in my life's endeavors, physically abused, verbally abused, emotionally abused, cheated on and once again forsaken! Not like Jesus on the cross when He said, *My God, why has thou forsaken me* because God raised Him up in three days with all power in His hands. My forsakenness was in every way left behind with no plans of returning, revisiting, reconciling nor supporting.

TD Jakes said it best, "There are people who can walk away from you. And hear me when I tell you this! When people can walk away from you, let them walk. I don't want you to try to talk another person into staying with you, loving you, calling you, caring about you, coming to see you, staying attached to you. Your destiny is never tied to anyone who leaves you, and it doesn't mean they are bad people. It just means that their part in your story is over."

The day he walked out, I thought it was the ultimate betrayal. Who walks out on their family and not look back? I recall the day it happened so clearly.

How it all started with Carl?

As we communicated more and hung out weekly, we grew fond of each other. He was another tall, good looking man and charming, in his own way. He learned my work schedule and that I wasn't a young woman of the streets. I went to work, picked my child up from school, went home to cook and do homework with my son. The doorbell would ring shortly after I got home and it would be Carl. He was there so frequently after work for hours that I would often ask when he was going home. He would allude to staying and I would send him home only for him to return the next day. I'm unsure why I felt the need to get married in four months, but he asked, and I accepted. He didn't have a full-time job, a working vehicle or a place of his own. Today, that is a huge red flag for me, for sure! We got married and of course, he moved in, with nothing but his clothes.

Although I lived in my parent's home, I still paid my father a "stipend". Somehow, when the two of us got married, we didn't always have the money to pay…

probably because we were hanging out and spending money unnecessarily and regularly. I was never the type to hang-out, but you wouldn't have known it after we got together. Carl would never call to talk to my father, man to man. He would always have me ask for the pardon on the "stipend".

In this home is where the things started happening; arguments that led to him putting his hands on me. My oldest son would come to my rescue and he would threaten him. Here is where the secrets began. In fear of my son getting hurt, I told him not to worry about me because I was okay and not to tell anyone anything that happened in our house. I was protecting him from protecting me. Today, I can't imagine what he went through hearing the arguments and the abuse. My heart goes out to him just reminiscing about it. Even though we argued a lot, I thought it was somewhat normal for most couples. In the midst of it all, we were trying to conceive a baby, but we were unsuccessful - in the beginning. I finally conceived after more than a year of trying and gave premature birth to another beautiful son, Andre. He was a little over three pounds but a fighter. He stayed in the hospital for 10 days, then he came home with me, healthy and thriving.

Still home on maternity leave, one morning while resting, a woman called. She said that she was Carl's girlfriend. Stunned, I sat straight up in the bed. She boldly told me who she was, that she worked at the barber school he attended and when I would page him and he didn't respond, it was because he was with her. I hung the phone up on her several times and she kept calling back. Before cell phones were common, we used pagers to communicate. I paged Carl to call home and when he did, I was frantic. I went to the school immediately and the policemen were there questioning him. Evidently, he had approached the woman while she was putting some things in the trunk of her car. He asked her why she called me. She laughed at him, so he shoved her into the trunk and slammed it closed. Someone released the trunk lock for her to breakout and she called the police. When they arrived, she told the officers that Carl had stolen money from her. He was instructed to pay it back or be arrested. He gave her the money; however, they both had to give a statement and appear in court. On the court date, the woman didn't show up. Fortunately for Carl, the judge thought it was comical and dismissed the case. The day after this incident, he confessed everything to me. I was disappointed and hurt. The next day, we went to his brother's house but I was really sad, so I sat in the car with the door opened, my legs were on the outside. When Carl realized I was still hurt, he became angry and tried to slam the car door on my legs. Quick reflexes allowed me to partially stop the impact with my hands but it still hit my legs. This cycle of events continued throughout our marriage and I became very intimidated and fearful of him.

A couple of years later, my parents relocated back home, and we moved out of their house into our own apartment. I remember my mom saying it looked like someone kicked the bedroom door open. I, of course, pretended as though I didn't know what she was talking about and denied it. There were many nights I had locked myself in the bedroom or the bathroom at our other home because I was afraid of him. When Andre' was a toddler, he would knock on the bathroom door to let him in. I was afraid to open the door thinking Carl would be standing there. When I did open the door, Andre' would sit with me in the bathroom until I thought it was safe to come out. Carl would get so angry, and although I never gave him permission to put his hands on me, he thought it was okay to do so. I only recall him punching me once in the back of my head, knocking my glasses off my face. Any other time, he would push, shove, hold me down, squeeze my hands forcefully and lay his dead weight on me while holding my hands above my head firmly. It was difficult to move and the more I tried to get loose, the tighter he squeezed my hands, held my arms down and the more weight he would apply on me. I would go into a panic feeling as though I couldn't breathe but learned how to resort to prayer with my eyes closed for God's peace until he was ready to release me.

Things didn't change much as the years went by. We moved into a home and I found myself locking myself in the bathroom again to escape the long nights of agony. I often knew what kind of night I would have when he walked through the door from work. I would usually be in the kitchen cooking or finishing dinner. If he walked in talking, whistling or singing, we were going to have a good night. If he walked in, shut the door and there was no response to hello, I was in for a hell of a night. I remember telling him that one of these nights he was going to really hurt me and he would often say he was just playing. The joke was at my expense. Enduring all of this, we were workers in our church and business owners. People loved him and if they saw one of us they saw us both. Funny how you can look churchy and happy but behind closed doors, no one knows the struggle.

Fast forwarding, my youngest son was in the second grade when Carl began to really pull away. He started hanging out, smoking and drinking with those who worked in our shop. Yes, our shop. I was a silent owner because he was on the check system and couldn't get a bank account without my signature. The atmosphere at our business changed because of this and he started losing business. He placed chairs on the side of the building where they would take breaks to smoke and drink. Inside he played R-rated movies. We had a routine of taking the kids for pizza on Friday evenings but he stopped coming home after work to hang out with his friends. One day, he told me that he didn't want to live for anyone anymore; he wanted to just do what he wanted to and live for himself. I didn't know what he meant by that but I advised him that he should do what makes him happy. Little did I know that meant he was no longer happy with me. Shortly after that, he warned me that he would be going out every weekend and I needed to learn how to pay the bills, as we shared bank accounts but he made the payments, and he would not be answering phone calls from me any longer. He didn't waste any time on putting that into action. The next weekend, he did just what he said. He didn't come home after work, and he didn't answer my calls. This went on for a few months. One evening he asked me to meet him for dinner. As we sat and talked he told me that he no longer loved me and wanted a divorce. Hurt and devastated, I said nothing and left him sitting in the restaurant.

After that night, I no longer wanted to go home after work. I would pick the kids up, go to my parents' house and stay until it was the kids' bedtime. I would still get home before he did and he retreated to sleeping on the sofa. Carl's emotional distance grew to the point that he packed a bag and would be gone the entire weekend. Then the weekend turned into a week. When he returned, he would never unpack his bag. He kept it in the truck until he was ready to disappear again. One morning, I mustered the courage to tell Carl that I was leaving for work and would see him later. He said to me that when I come home, he would no longer be there. He got up, went to the closet and began to remove the remainder of his clothes taking them to the new truck that I just bought. His credit was too low to finance, so I did. When he removed all of what he wanted, leaving remnants on the floor of the closet, he pulled items from the drawers until he had enough. I stood and watched him go back and forth and asked if we could talk. He replied that I should have talked the night before when he came in after 3am. If I stood in his way, he would have walked over me like a freight train on the track with a mission. I stood at the door as he got into the truck, backed out of the driveway and drove off. I asked God, what do I do now? I pulled myself together, got my kids up and dropped them off to school. He wouldn't return my phone calls and when he did answer at the shop, he would cuss me out and call me out of my name. It didn't matter how nice I tried to be, he would always disrespect me and hang the phone up. I would call back every time until one day, I stopped. I was tired of being hung up on, so I stopped. He noticed the change and began to call me every once in a while just to keep his foot in the door. Andre's birthday was approaching and he asked me to meet him at Sam's Club for some of the birthday items and to give me Andre's gift. He had been estranged for a while and I was really just over it. While walking through the store, he began to pull on and touch me inappropriately. I demanded him to stop but he continued until we got to the register. At this point, I was so irritated and mortified, so I told him if he couldn't come home to be my husband that he didn't need to be pulling and tugging on me. We checked out and he was angry at that statement. I drove to where he was parked and he placed the gift and items in my vehicle. I was standing at the driver's door arguing with him when he began to back up with the door opened. I was about to be dragged if I didn't move out of the way. I panicked and slammed his door shut and asked if he was trying to run me over. He was upset that I slammed his door closed and followed me to another store, jumped out of the truck and pushed me against the outside wall with his hands around my neck and rambling. As he walked away from me, I told him that I was coming to get the truck because he wasn't making payments on it and it was messing up my credit. He told me to come get it and when I did, he ran out of our shop with a gun propped on his side like he was a gangster in a western movie, insisting that I get out of the truck. He shot the gun in the air above the truck and I halted. My sons were in the car in front of me and I motioned for them to keep going. I wanted them to get out of harm's way. Within minutes, a SWAT team was surrounding the shop. They questioned both of us about what had occurred. He told them that I wasn't his wife and that we just lived together. No one in the shop vouched for me; they protected him and said they didn't hear a gun shot or knew what was going on. The vehicle's registration was in my name so he was ordered to relinquish it to me. While asleep that night, he came and confiscated the vehicle. Once again, I was in the same position as I struggled with the why is this happening and how did this happen to me. However, if he had never left, I probably would have stayed in that mess. Meantime, because our home was purchased based on two incomes, I couldn't afford to make the payments. When he left, he didn't look back. I had to figure out how to feed my kids, keep the utilities on and pay my mortgage. I was too prideful to ask my parents, therefore, I couldn't make the mortgage payments, so the foreclosure process began. It was feast or famine. My kids had to eat and we needed running water and electricity. I was so broken and numb. I didn't know if I would ever feel normal or happy again. One day while driving home from work, I wanted to be out of my misery and pain and thus contemplated letting go of the steering wheel, closing my eyes and releasing the car to go into the wall. As much as I wanted to, the Holy Spirit wouldn't let me take my hands off of the steering wheel. I was so distraught and I didn't know what to do, except cry out to the Lord and He kept me and strengthened me. A few days later, I was driving home from picking Jon up from work and he said to me, "sometimes you have to step back and a let God bless you to move forward"... and a little child shall lead them (Isaiah 11:6). Those words brought encouragement to me. I decided to let go and let God lead me. I heard God's voice through him and trusted His guidance. Weeping may endure for a night but joy comes in the morning, Psalm 30:5. The sun was beginning to shine.

Six

My kids and I transitioned into an apartment complex not too far from where we were living to keep Jon in the same school. It was his senior year of high school and I didn't want to uproot him in the middle of the school year. Andre' had a difficult time accepting the move and his father's absence. He began to struggle in school, emotionally and academically, that year. He was missing his father and was heartbroken about the separation. He would often spend weekends with his dad and he looked forward to it but one particular weekend Carl did not answer Andre's phone calls. On the way home from school, he asked to stop by because he really wanted to spend time with his dad. We pulled up and he went to the door. His father answered and said he could still stay but his girlfriend was in town and staying with him. At the time, he only had one bedroom set and Andre' slept with him. I told him that Andre' was uncomfortable seeing him with another woman and with him behind closed doors so it was best to reschedule their time for another weekend and he agreed. On the drive home, Andre' and I both were silently crying and half way there I explained to him that he was loved by both of us although his father and I were not together; that if he wanted the best possible and happy dad, we have to accept what makes him happy. I told him that I was okay and I wanted him to be okay and suggested that we get all of the crying out right now and we were never going to cry over that situation again. I promised him that we were going to be okay, I had his back and I was going to make sure he had everything he needed. And I gave him my word that home would always be home and he would never have to ask if he can come home. We cried all the way home. The next day, Andre' was okay but I was still hurting. He received it and let it go.

The problem was, I was still stuck but pretended to be okay, as I've always done. I realized that I was keeping Andre' stuck by showing my emotions and I wanted him to be free. I drew my strength from my son, instead of him drawing it from me. God showed

Himself through my son and my healing began. Throughout it all, I relied on prayer, and reading God's Word to sustain me. I attended the Women's Sunday school class at my church and was so emotionally distressed that I couldn't comprehend the lesson. Nevertheless, I kept pressing until I started enjoying the bible studies. I got so involved that it felt as though I was in the book and part of the storyline. It was a year of growth. So much had happened that the year that it was a mist in my memory. It was time to renew my lease and when I did, the Lord spoke to my spirit and said not to renew it a second time. I didn't understand because I had an active foreclosure on my credit report and I was now a single income household. I began to believe God more and more as the year went by. I didn't know how to get started but when we don't understand the Lord steps in and does what He does best, make it happen. He tells us in Proverbs 3:5-6 to trust in the Lord with all of our hearts and lean not to our own understanding. In all our ways acknowledge Him and He will direct our paths.

About six months later an email appeared in my box to attend a first time home buyer's workshop. I work at a hospital and thought it was really strange to receive an email regarding non-hospital affairs. I read it and immediately dismissed it thinking I didn't qualify because number one, I had a foreclosure on my credit file and I didn't make enough money. How many of us know that God is a God of more than enough? About a week went by and the same email came back that a first time homebuyer's workshop would be held as a one-day seminar on-campus. This time, I paused and asked God out loud, what are you trying to tell me? There was no way I would be excused from work for a full day to attend a session on-campus regarding a topic that has nothing to do with my job. However, I decided to ask my manager for the day off to attend a meeting on-site. I told her what it was about and she said sure and gave me the day off with pay. This is just the beginning; put your seatbelt on. I wasn't ready and didn't understand how God was about to bless me but I prayed and asked God to go before me.

I arrived at the building and as I entered the elevator, a vibrant and very happy young lady entered along with me and said hello. I quietly returned the greeting because I was unsure of what I was about to walk into. She then asked where I was going and I told her. She said, good, me too and I'm a loan officer. At that time, I didn't know what a loan officer meant but I felt a little connection. The first half focused on the preparation of buying a home. For example, making sure your credit report and score was good and eliminating unnecessary debt. We broke for lunch and when I returned everyone was lined up to meet individually with a loan officer. I was a little disappointed because the man sitting beside me was next in line, which meant he would meet with the lender that I met in the elevator. When it was his turn, he passed and said he was waiting for someone else. Guess who's up? Me! She said to follow her and as I entered the office, I blurted that I didn't know why I was there because I have a foreclosure and I didn't qualify. Her response was, *ye of little faith.* I felt like it was the Lord chastising me. I walked out of there qualified for $75,000 thirteen years ago! I was so excited and grateful to God that I would have been able to buy a townhouse for my sons and me.

A few days later I received a call from the loan officer that reviewed my loan request to notify me that the bank had increased my loan amount to $125,000! Amazing, but I didn't know the challenges of purchasing a home. First of all, my realtor was too busy to assist me in finding a home. Therefore, I would pack my sons up in my car after work every evening to drive through neighborhoods looking for a house. To no avail, I couldn't find a house in my price range. I quickly found out that $125,000 was not enough to find a home in a nice neighborhood where I felt comfortable. I remember praying to God asking him to send someone to help me because I know He had a house for me. Well, God does answer prayers. We ask and don't always recognize it when God sends help our way. I was so exhausted trying to find a house with no success and still going through the motions of a failed marriage. One evening that same week, Andre' had a football game. He had to be at the field an hour early. I sat in the truck, tired, depressed and not wanting to talk to anyone. Somehow when our backs are against the wall and we don't have the answers or nowhere else to turn, God provides a ram in the bush. As I looked up, a young lady named Robin passed by looking for a parking spot and waived when she saw me. The Holy Spirit was urging me to get out of the truck. I kept saying, I don't want to get out but it was impressed in me stronger and stronger to get out. I said, I'll get out but I'm standing by my car because I don't want to talk to anyone. Robin approached me and asked how I was doing. For some reason, I spilled everything to her. *I'm going through a divorce and was qualified for a home, but I can't find a nice house for my children and I in a nice neighborhood.* She calmly asked what loan amount I was approved for. When I told her, she said she works with developers and they build houses in new neighborhoods. I asked her what part of $125,000 she didn't understand. She replied that this is a God thing and, therefore, I humbled myself. I took a drive with her through a new subdivision and asked if I could live there. She reminded me that this is a God thing so my perspective changed. The houses were over my preapproved amount but Robin spoke to the construction manager, that I still haven't met today, and he automatically reduced the price of the home by $8,000. However, I was still short by $9,000! I didn't know where this money was coming from. I was so nervous that they approved my application and I didn't have the funds for the remaining balance, down payment or closing costs. I bombarded God for answers and He kept telling me to trust Him. The clock was ticking and I was getting closer to the closing date. I told God I didn't understand where the money was coming from. He said don't ask the church, don't ask my parents and don't ask anyone. I said to Him that I just didn't know how I was going to get it. Was it going to drop from the sky into my account?? Was I going to open my mailbox and it would be in there? Lord, I don't understand. I started praying, Lord, I believe but please help my unbelief. My loan officer didn't have faith in me getting this house and had her husband, who is a Realtor, send me active listings. Every listing I clicked on to view had expired or was no longer available. I cried out to the Lord that I didn't understand. He was sending me back to this house but I didn't have the money. I was like, okay, Lord, I trust You.

One day Robin called and told me that she had scheduled an appointment for me. I didn't ask her what the appointment was for but I trusted her and went to the appointment. As I walked in, the young lady said she heard I would be coming in jumping and leaping. I replied that I just came to see what God was going to do. She escorted me to her office and later told me she went to pray for God to show her what I needed. When she re-entered the office, she explained that her company provides grants for various things and asked me to fill out an application that took about 10 minutes to complete. She looked over it for about a minute and said approved! She said, they just happen to have $9,000 remaining just for me. It was a forgivable loan, meaning I didn't have to pay it back. I was so excited and in amazement that I kept saying to her, you just don't understand, this is a God thing! I couldn't wait to get back to my office to call my loan officer to tell her my good news. By the time I called her, the grant office had already contacted her. She told me they changed their minds and didn't give me the $9,000 after all. My heart dropped and I asked what happened? She said, well I told them that you needed the money for closing costs, as well so they gave you $13,000! Let me tell you, God is so amazing! Who needs silver and gold when you have God on your side?

I wasted no time notifying the office of the apartment complex that I would not be renewing my lease because I was working on purchasing a house. She suggested that I renew just in case it didn't go through securing a place for me and if things did work out, I can cancel the lease. I agreed and signed the lease. Once I found out that everything was working out with the new home, I called the office to notify them to cancel my lease. I didn't remember who I had spoken to but to my surprise I was told that I couldn't break a lease because it's a legal contract binding me to fulfill the obligations of the agreement. Thus, for me to get out of the contract, I would have to pay for the remaining months. Unbelievable, right? I calmly asked if I could come to the office to talk with her and she agreed. I picked Andre' up from school and as I backed in the parking space, I asked God to go before me. I went into the office and told them who I was and that I had spoken to someone about my lease renewal. She got up to get my file but could not locate it. She looked in every drawer, cabinet, trash cans and papers on her desk but could not find it. She was exhausted and said it was like I had never been a tenant there. I looked over my shoulder and whispered, Thank you, God!"

She apologized and pulled out a new contract for me sign but I told her I would not be renewing and that I was submitting my notice to vacate. I walked out there in awe of an awesome God.

God never ceases to amaze me. I had put $800 earnest money down on my new home but Robin told me that the builder said I could not get that money back because of the reduction in the building cost they afforded me. I was okay with that. My closing was scheduled for December 6th, Jon's birthday. I told my sons that there would be no Christmas gifts that year because my money went into buying the house. They said okay with no concern about Christmas gifts and went back to doing what they were doing. That following Sunday in church, my former Pastor, Dr. Augustus D. Robinson, Jr., preached a sermon as though he had walked my path. It mirrored everything I went through to get this home. He preached on how God will send someone to you when your back is against the wall and you don't know where to turn, when people turn their backs on you and leave you, when husbands walk out on you, God has a plan. The more he preached, the more the Holy Spirit was saying in my spirit to get up and tell someone. I didn't want to but I was so compelled to go although fighting it. I don't hear an audible voice but I always hear the Lord speak loudly in my spirit and I was telling Him "No" in my spirit. Lord, you will have to make me go.

Andre' was about 10 years old at the time. He turned to me and said, "Mama, you need to tell your story."

I was so shocked. It was as though he could hear my conversation with the Lord. I told him, No. He pulled my arm saying, "Yes Mama, you have to tell your story!"

I told him if he didn't stop pulling on me, I was going to spank him. The lady next to him asked if I needed to get out and I softly said, "Yes."

Andre' and I went to the front of the church after the sermon was preached. Pastor Robinson opened the doors of the church for salvation, testimonies, to join a ministry, etc. I remember it was a first Sunday. The announcements are brief because the Lord's Supper (Communion) is served. Pastor Robinson came to me with the mic, but I told him that I had changed my mind.

Puzzled, he asked, "What?"

I whispered, "I changed my mind, Pastor".

He placed the mic back to my mouth and said, "You can do it!"

I mustered through it, but I got it all out how my husband left us, I lost my home and the Lord told me not to renew my lease. I explained how I didn't know how but God sent someone to me and I would be closing on a brand new home soon. Everyone celebrated with me and I felt so good to testify about what God had done for me. My brothers and sisters embraced and congratulated me as I exited the Sanctuary. Pastor Robinson is a true man of God. He preached that and many other sermons as led by God, touching, changing, and transforming lives through the power of God. He counseled me through many difficult times while going through my separation and divorce. I still remember some of the scriptures he gave to me to meditate on, such as, Isaiah 40:31. They that wait upon the Lord shall renew their strength; they shall mount up with wings of eagles. They shall run and not be weary, walk and not faint.

A friend, Jackie Starks, came to me and said, "Read this!" I forgot that we both had written what we wanted God to do for us the previous year. We exchanged the letters and placed them in our bibles in Habakkuk 2:2, "write the vision and make it plain..."

I opened the letter that I had written how I was believing and thanking God for my new 3-bedroom, 2 bathroom and 1 car garage home.

Jackie kept that letter and God had answered my prayers! I was so taken back as I read it seeing how God made a way out of no way for me and how He honored my prayer. I just got the chills thinking about it.

The day of closing, I anxiously went to the attorney's office. A young lady came from the back and apologized that they had to reschedule because the check came in for a different amount that was on the closing document. They sent a check for $15,000 not $13,000! She asked if I could come back the next day and of course I agreed. I am more than blown away, I'm feeling all of God's favor because I could see how God was restoring the years that the locust had eaten. Joel 2:25 "Of course, I'll come back tomorrow!" The next day, I went into the closing and signed a hundred documents. At the very end, Robin said, "We have something for you."

It was my $800 earnest money! I cried and thanked God and thanked God and cried. I almost wet my pants. I had to be excused to the ladies room. My sons could have a Christmas after all!

Somebody prayed for me, had me on their minds, took the time and prayed for me. I'm so glad they prayed. I'm so glad they prayed. I'm so glad they prayed for me!

God had me on His mind. We lived there for 10 years and I finished raising my sons in that home.

Seven ... Purpose

Jon graduated from high school. Initially, he planned to go away to college but he decided to stay here to help me because I was going through a divorce and he was worried about my well-being. I told him I would be okay but he insisted. He received a full scholarship to a local college and work-study on the Charleston Air Force Base. I was so very proud of him and humbled that he put himself aside for his mother. He was able to purchase a car on his own and become a responsible young adult. I admired how he went to school and worked while his peers went off to school. However, he didn't honor it and lost the scholarship, which meant he lost the job. How many of us know that through our failures God has a way of reaching way down to pick us up? Well, as difficult as it is to get a job at one of the largest hospitals in South Carolina, the doors were opened for him. One day I was in the Human Resources office taking care of some business when one of the recruiters leaned back in her chair to speak to me. When I warmly smiled and greeted her, she told me that there was a patient transporter's position available. I was confused because I certainly didn't want to push beds and wheelchairs with patients in them all over the hospital. I just said, "Really – ok." Not knowing that Jon had just lost his job, she asked if he would be interested. I suddenly understood and answered quickly and directly, "Yes, he is interested!"

I ensured that he completed the application process that day and she referred him to the hiring manager. Without a formal interview, he got the job. Isaiah 55:8 says, "For my thoughts are not your thoughts, neither are your ways my ways, saith the Lord."

Jon worked in transportation for a short period before he was noticed by the clinical staff in the Surgical Trauma Intensive Care Unit. His reputation preceded him as a young man with great work ethics, that's respectful and very dependable. They offered him a patient tech position, and paid for schooling to get his certification. He passed the course with an A. They held the job for him and hired him after the completion of the course. He worked there for four years and excelled in that area so well, 10 years later, the staff still asks me about him. He transitioned from the hospital and enlisted in the US Navy and once again excelled. He met his beautiful wife, Markita, and they have been married for nine years. To their union they were blessed with three amazingly gorgeous and smart children, (my grandkids) Jon Michael Jr. 8 years old, Ari Samiya 5 years old and Nia Malika 11 months old. He was recently promoted and will be relocated to Washington, DC working as the Presidential Ceremonial Guard. Markita will be continuing her career in Culinary Arts. She is an amazing and crafty cake designer, cookies and all types of beautifully designed treats. I have always prayed over and with my kids that God blesses everything their hands touches, everywhere their feet trods and all that they say and do. I've watched God bless their life's paths and guide them into their purpose. All things work together for the good of them that love the Lord, those who are the called according to His purpose. Romans 8:28

Andre' is ten years younger than Jon. He wasn't very happy about Jon enlisting in the military and it took a while for him to adjust to just being with me. As close as I am to my children, Andre 'and I had to figure out how to live without Jon in the home. He was always involved in sports and my life was centered on taking him to track, football and baseball practice and games. He played on the number one football team all through high school and began receiving scholarships to play in college his senior year. With three games left in the season, he was hit pretty hard in one of the games. He was laid up and taken out of the game. He had been down many times during his football career but this time was different. As soon as he was hit, I knew something was wrong. I never run on the field, but I did that night. Before returning to practice and games, he had to be seen by a sports medicine physician. He was anxious to get cleared for practice that Wednesday so he could play in the Thursday game that would be aired on television. He reminded me over and over to call and get his results from the doctor but before I could call, the doctor called me by 7 a.m. I was not prepared to hear the news he shared with me. Andre' has congenital spinal stenosis and should not have ever played contact sports. They strongly advised that he discontinued playing forever.

Wow, what a blow. How do I tell my son this devastating news? I called his father and then the school to ensure they did not tell him. I was on the way to the school to tell him myself. His father and I met the football coaches and Andre' was called to the office. As he entered the office, I could see the joy and excitement on his face thinking he had received a big athletic scholarship. As he sat, everyone was in silence until I spoke up gently and as lovingly as a hurt parent reveals disappointing news to her child. Needless to say, he was floored and it took three months before he started feeling better.

In the midst of all of his disappointment, I called in the men leaders from the church to pray and encourage him. Deacon DeShean Garrett was one of the three that faithfully came to pray, share and encourage him. The prayers impacted his life to press on through by applying for colleges and accepting that God still has a plan for his life. While working, he tried the pharmacy and nursing programs at a local college but they were not good fits for him. Everyone's path is not the same... he followed in his brother's footsteps and worked as a patient transporter at the same hospital for four years. He decided to take a different route and received his lean manufacturing certification that opened the doors for him to get a good job at a prominent plant. This blessing afforded him the opportunity at 22 years old to have his first home built. For I know the plans I have for you, declares the Lord, plans to prosper you and not harm you, plans to give you hope and a future. Jeremiah 29:11

Now that my sons are doing well, it's time for Mama to walk her journey. At this point, I've purchased two new homes, two reliable vehicles, received my Master's Degree, Real Estate License, currently writing two books, walking in my purpose in ministry and working out my salvation with fear and trembling.

The year 2018 was definitely the year of new beginnings and purpose for my family and for me. For years, God has shown me the number 810, especially, when He is about to do something new in my life. When I first started seeing the number years ago, I would look up scripture to see if I would get a revelation. Nehemiah 8:10... *the joy of the Lord is my strength* stuck with me. I began to make positive confessions to myself every morning, such as, I am fearfully and wonderfully made, my comings and goings are blessed, no weapon that is formed against me shall prosper, and I'm more than a conqueror through Christ Jesus who loves me. Today, I still make those confessions and it keeps me and reminds me of whom I am in Christ Jesus. I've been employed at the hospital for 27 years giving me retirement eligibility in October this year.

After receiving my Master's Degree, the doors didn't open for promotion immediately. I didn't understand and became discouraged. Last year a co-worker and friend, Jules Kohler, suggested that I apply for a promotable position. I declined and told her I would just ride my time out - but she insisted and allowed God to use her. I applied, and after five formal and one informal interview, I was the number one candidate of 50 applicants. Incredible! Jules kept saying, "you got this!" and I began to believe God for it more and more. Sixteen months before retirement eligibility, I got a new job in **June**. The job I desired to have. For with God nothing shall be impossible Luke 1:37.

In **July**, Andre' got a new job and I was blessed with my 3rd grandchild, Nia. In **August**, Jon was meritoriously promoted and Markita graduated from Culinary Arts School. Now unto Him that is able to do exceeding abundantly above all that we ask or think, according to the power that works in us... Ephesians 3:20.

I now realize that what God allowed was for my good and for His glory. You see, God never left me nor did he forsake me. It may appear that there was trouble on every side from what I recall. However, it was a setback, an event that delays your progress or reverses some of the progress you have made. God was divinely setting me up. For it was His plan for a comeback, recovery or return to my former position or state of mind. John 10:10 says, the thief comes not, but for to steal, to kill and to destroy. I come that they might have life, and that they might have it more abundantly.

I'm thanking God for strong and loving parents that introduced me to Christ as a child. If it had not been for the Lord on my side, I don't know where I would be. In my darkest hours, I called on Him and he heard me, kept me, comforted me and saved me. I didn't know the Lord the way I do today but I knew that He could keep a secret. Throughout the years, my fear of opening my mouth imprisoned me. I once allowed people to take advantage of me by accepting their bad behavior, belittling me, discarding and disrespecting me. Today, I know that God has given me many gifts to walk in and to share with others. The future is not just ahead of me, it was birthed inside of me. God has not given us the spirit of fear, but of love, power and of a sound mind. What God has given to us, the world cannot take it away.

People may try to destroy through their evil tactics, but know that we are more than conquerors through Christ Jesus who loves us, and we can do all things through Christ who strengthens us. Your outcome is not determined by your current circumstances. God has a plan for each of our lives, and if we draw close to Him, He will draw close to us. Just ask and believe and you will receive all that God has for you. The LORD is thy keeper: the LORD is thy shade upon thy right hand (Psalm 121:5).

We may be troubled on every side, yet not distressed; we are perplexed, but not in despair, persecuted, but not forsaken; cast down, but not destroyed (2 Corinthians 4:8-9).

My one and only favorite poem, *Our Deepest Fear*, written by Marianne Williamson, has been an encouragement in knowing that our deepest fear is not that we are inadequate but are powerful beyond measure. It is our light, not our darkness that most frightens us. I love how it asks, who am I to be brilliant, gorgeous, talented, and fabulous? Then reminds us that we are a child of God and playing small does not serve the world. Know that there's nothing enlightened by shrinking so that other people won't feel insecure around you. It closes by saying as we let our own light shine, we unconsciously give other people permission to do the same and as we are liberated from our own fear, our presence automatically liberate others.

As I grew closer to God and in His grace, I didn't know how to accept complements and would often downplay the good things that were happening to and for me; all the doors that God was opening and the doors that He was closing. Today, I am no longer apologetic for the blessings that God has bestowed upon me. I realize that as I downplayed my accomplishments, I was actually discarding the call on my life and the many blessings from God. Knowing that the Word in I Samuel says, *for them that honor me I will honor, and they that despise me shall be lightly esteemed and if a man purges himself from these, he shall be a vessel unto honor, sanctified, and meet for the master's use, and prepared unto every good work.* Therefore, I graciously and humbly give God all of the Glory, all of the honor and all of the praise!

There is purpose for your pain and *God is nigh to all who have a contrite spirit.* It is a continuous process to become the person God wants us to be. See, our trials are not just meant for us. It is to learn from them, build character, to learn to trust God in all things and to be able to help someone else; to give our testimony of how we made it by the grace of God; how God kept us, comforted us and never left us alone because He has a plan for our lives.

It was only through the Grace of God that I survived. So, don't give up or give in. Keep pressing, praying and seeking God for guidance, deliverance, wisdom, knowledge and understanding. He will rescue, restore and set you free. You may not understand the process but lean not to your own understanding and trust God in all thy ways and He will direct your path (Proverbs 3:5-6).

If I had not seen the goodness of the Lord in the land of the living, I would have fainted. I never lost my faith and because of my faith, I was saved by grace - my life, my soul, my mind and my spirit.

Full recovery from an attack to the heart is possible but only through the grace of God. The scar tissue that is formed because of the attack may hinder the complete function of the heart requiring important lifestyle changes. Initially, it protects and covers up the damages that occurred, interrupting the natural flow of the blood but because of the saving blood of Jesus, we are made whole. Our trials come to make us strong, build character and strengthen our hearts. Keep your heart with all diligence; for out of it are the issues of life. So speak life and step out in faith knowing that God hears and answers prayers.

If you or someone you may know is experiencing any type of abuse, contact a crimes victims advocate, the National Sexual Assault Online Hotline, The National Domestic Violence Hotline, or any National Hotline for support for Trauma or Abuse.

May the good Lord bless you and keep you, make His face shine upon you, and be gracious to you; lift up His countenance upon you, and give you peace. Amen!

About the Author

Sonja Pinckney Rhodes is a Young Adult Ministry Advisor, an Advisor of the Baptist Young Women, a Sunday school teacher, a Business Manager, and a Licensed Real Estate Agent. She has a BA in Human Resource Management and an MA in Business Management. She is the proud mother of two sons, a daughter-in-law, and three beautiful grandchildren.

Ms. Pinckney's first book, *Pain to Purpose*, was inspired by God to share how He had a plan for her life to prosper despite the obstacles she encountered on her journey. It gives helpful insight through her walk with God on how her broken pieces can be effective in the lives of others. The voice that was once stolen from her is now restored and heard through her teaching and writing.

Made in the USA
Middletown, DE
10 July 2019